THE BATTLES OF LEXINGTON AND CONCORD

Charlie Samuels

Gareth Stevens
Publishing

Please visit our website, www.garethstevens.com. For a free color catalog of all our high-quality books, call toll-free 1-800-542-2595 or fax 1-877-542-2596.

Library of Congress Cataloging-in-Publication Data

Samuels, Charlie.
The battles of Lexington and Concord / by Charlie Samuels.
 p. cm. — (Turning points in US history)
Includes index.
ISBN 978-1-4824-0418-0 (pbk.)
ISBN 978-1-4824-3313-5 (6-pack)
ISBN 978-1-4824-0417-3 (library binding)
1. Lexington, Battle of, Lexington, Mass., 1775 — Juvenile literature. 2. Concord, Battle of, Concord, Mass., 1775 — Juvenile literature. I. Samuels, Charlie, 1961- II. Title.
E241.L6 S26 2014
973.3311—dc23

Published in 2014 by
Gareth Stevens Publishing
111 East 14th Street, Suite 349
New York, NY 10003

© 2014 Brown Bear Books Ltd

For Brown Bear Books Ltd:
Editorial Director: Lindsey Lowe
Managing Editor: Tim Cooke
Children's Publisher: Anne O'Daly
Art Director: Keith Davis
Designer: Lynne Lennon
Picture Manager: Sophie Mortimer
Production Director: Alastair Gourlay

Picture Credits:
Front Cover: U.S. Army

All images Library of Congress except:
Topfoto: Granger Collection 25; **Carolyn A. & Peter S. Lynch Gallery:** 28; **Hohum:** 27; **Munson-Williams-Proctor Institute of Art:** 40; **Robert Hunt Library:** 19, 21; **Shutterstock:** Michael Borders 11, Jeffrey M. Frank 18, James Morgan 31; **Thinkstock:** istockphoto 38, Photos.com 7, 33; **U.S. Army:** 34, 35, 36; **White House Historical Association:** 37, 39.

All Artworks © Brown Bear Books Ltd

Brown Bear Books has made every attempt to contact the copyright holder. If you have any information please contact smortimer@brownbearbooks.co.uk

Manufactured in the United States of America

CPSIA compliance information: Batch #CW14GS. For further information contact Gareth Stevens, New York, New York at 1-800-542-2595.

CONTENTS

INTRODUCTION

The clashes between American militia and British redcoats that happened at Lexington and Concord, Massachusetts, on April 19, 1775, were not much more than skirmishes. They involved fewer men than there are students at many high schools. But their effect was as decisive as that of any fight between far larger forces. The thirteen colonies the British had set up in North America were now in armed rebellion against the king. The American Revolution, or Revolutionary War, had begun.

Anger and Rebellion

Lexington and Concord were the result of a long period in which colonial Americans had become increasingly angry about the government in London. Many Americans had fought with the British to defeat the French in Canada in the French and Indian War (1754–1763). But they came to believe that their colonial masters saw the Americas only as a source of income. They believed the government was denying them the same political freedoms enjoyed by the British in Britain. The militia at Lexington and Concord were volunteers who believed passionately that they were defending those freedoms against a tyrant: the British king, George III. Over the following years, these volunteers would become the basis of a highly effective fighting force.

British redcoats storm American patriot positions at Bunker Hill in June 1775. To begin with, the patriots found it difficult to defeat Britain's regular army.

This contemporary engraving by Cornelius Tiebout shows militia firing on the British at Lexington on April 19, 1775.

British America

At the start of the American Revolution, most Americans who took up arms against the British had little intention of creating an independent country. They were more interested in getting the British government to treat them in the same way in which the king's subjects were treated back in Britain.

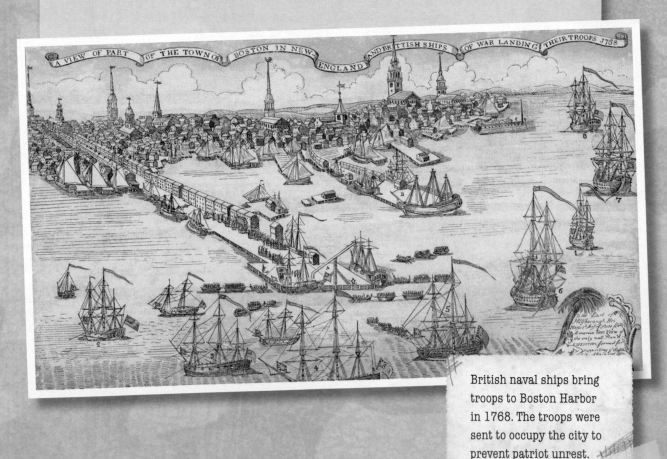

British naval ships bring troops to Boston Harbor in 1768. The troops were sent to occupy the city to prevent patriot unrest.

British warships defeat a Dutch fleet at the Battle of Camperdown in 1797. Britain's empire relied on its naval strength.

By the mid–18th century, the British had been settling in North America for some 150 years. The east coast was divided into thirteen British colonies stretching from Massachusetts in the north to Georgia in the south. In the north, the French claimed much of what is now Canada. Inland, they also claimed the Mississippi Valley.

Life in the Colonies

More than 1.6 million British subjects lived in colonial America by 1760. Most had never been to Britain; their families had moved to North America decades earlier. American society was thriving. Many colonists lived in busy cities such

THE BRITISH EMPIRE

North America was one of the largest regions of the growing British empire. Using the strength of the Royal Navy, the British held territory around Hudson Bay in Canada and on Caribbean islands. The British had also established trading posts in South America, West Africa, and South Asia. Over the next century, this network of posts would be the basis of an empire that stretched around the world—even though the British lost control of the United States.

At the end of the American Revolution, in 1783, Boston built a new State House to replace the one the British had used.

as Philadelphia, New York, and Boston. North America had its own road network and mail service, schools and universities, cathedrals, newspapers, and businesses. Meanwhile, farmers used the countryside to grow food and brave settlers moved into new lands on the frontier as British territory expanded. All these colonists were subject to the government in London, where King George III came to the British throne on October 25, 1760.

War with the French

By 1760 the stability of the colonies was threatened, and the frontier had become even more dangerous than usual. The colonists were at war with their French neighbors in a

KING GEORGE III

The reign of King George III, which began in 1760, was marked by conflict as European powers expanded their empires. When his subjects in America complained about their treatment by Parliament, George ignored them. To Americans, he was a tyrant who wanted to deprive them of their rights. Later in his reign, a blood disease caused him to become insane. In 1810 George was replaced by his son, George, Prince of Wales, who ruled as his father's regent.

George III—shown here in 1761, after he had come to the throne—is widely seen as handling the crisis in America very badly.

conflict known as the French and Indian War (1754–1763), because the various Native American peoples of the northeast took sides with either the French or the British. The war was just part of the Seven Years' War, a global struggle for power fought mainly between France and Britain as they attempted to extend their colonial rule. In North America, the British were eventually victorious, taking control of French territory in Canada and the Mississippi Valley. But that victory would only build up trouble for the future.

American Grievances

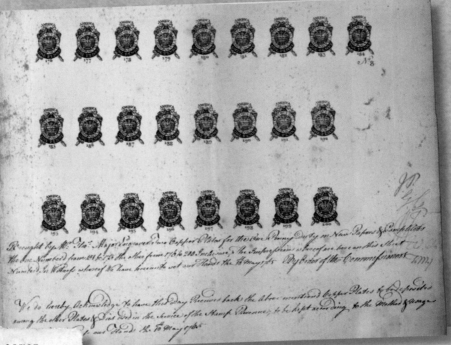

The Stamp Act of 1765 meant that every official document had to bear stamps to show that tax had been paid on it.

By the middle of the 18th century, some colonial Americans felt remote from their British rulers. After the French and Indian War, a series of extremely unpopular measures by the British convinced many Americans that things needed to change.

Most people in the thirteen colonies saw themselves as British subjects governed by Britain. Britain was their most important trade partner. The ports were full of British ships. British troops had protected them in the war.

Colonial Rights

At the same time, some colonists believed that Britain was so far away its government did not really understand North America. They resented the royal Proclamation of 1763, which forbade settlement west of the Appalachian Mountains. To make matters worse, in order to pay for the defense of the thirteen colonies, the British

The Appalachian Mountains were the western limit of the colonies. The Proclamation of 1763 forbade settlement farther west.

THE PROCLAMATION OF 1763

At the end of the French and Indian War, the British took control of Canada and the Mississippi Valley from France. George III issued a proclamation that forbade British settlement west of the Appalachian Mountains. He wanted to encourage settlement to the north, in Canada, and south—not in the west. In addition, the British were reluctant to provoke clashes with Native Americans on the frontier.

taxed their American subjects. The Americans complained because they had no members of Parliament to represent them in London. They said there should be "no taxation without representation." Groups called the Sons of Liberty formed in many colonies to protest against the British.

Taxes and Protests

In 1765, the British prime minister, George Grenville, imposed a stamp duty. Every official document or newspaper in British America had to be printed on paper that had been taxed.

The act was very unpopular. Eventually, mainly for reasons connected with British politics, it was repealed in 1766. In Massachusetts, colonial leader Samuel Adams wrote a letter

This cartoon shows Bostonians protesting the Stamp Act. The city was at the heart of protest against the British measures.

THE FRUITS OF ARBITRARY POWER, OR THE BLOODY MASSACRE PERPETRATED IN KING STREET BOSTON ON MARCH 5 1770. IN WHICH MESS.R SAM.L GRAY, SAM.L MAVERICK, JAMES CALDWELL, CRISPUS ATTUCKS, PATRICK CARR, WERE KILLED, SIX OTHER WOUNDED TWO OF THEM MORTALLY.

A painting of the Boston Massacre was turned into this engraving by the famed Boston patriot and silversmith, Paul Revere.

THE BOSTON MASSACRE

On March 5, 1770, a British soldier and a Bostonian began an argument in King Street. Soon an angry crowd surrounded the soldier. By the time other soldiers arrived to rescue him, they faced 400 or 500 protestors. The British held their fire, but the mob taunted them until one of the British fired. More shots rang out. As the smoke cleared, three Americans were dead—two more would soon die from their injuries.

that urged Americans not to cooperate with the British. In reaction, British troops occupied the Massachusetts capital, Boston. In 1770, troops opened fire on anti-British protestors in what was known as the Boston Massacre.

Patriotic Committees

Patriots set up Committees of Correspondence in 1772. Patriot leaders wrote to one another throughout the colonies to share ideas about government. In 1774, the patriots established Committees of Safety to monitor and report on the activities of the British colonial governments.

The Boston Tea Party

The Boston Tea Party was no tea party. It was the climax of protests by colonial Americans against British taxes. On December 16, 1773, citizens boarded British ships anchored in Boston Harbor, seized 340 chests of tea, and threw them overboard. It was a clear act of rebellion.

This illustration shows Bostonians cheering as the protestors—badly dressed as Native Americans—throw the tea overboard.

THE BOSTON TEA PARTY

The men who threw the tea overboard dressed as Mohawk to symbolize that their sympathy lay with America, not Britain.

The Bostonians were responding to a series of new taxes imposed by the British Parliament. The Sugar Act (1764), the Stamp Act (1765), and the Townshend Acts (1767) introduced new taxes on everyday items in the colonies.

A Costly Cup of Tea

After American protests, the British repealed the taxes, except the one on tea. When the Americans smuggled in Dutch tea, the British cut the cost of tea from India, another of their colonies. Indian tea flooded the market. The Tea Party was the Bostonians' way of objecting to what they saw as an illegal monopoly.

TROUBLE IN BOSTON

Boston was a major focus of the protest against British taxes. The city was an important port, and the taxes hurt its merchants badly. The Townshend Acts, for example, placed duty on goods made in Britain then exported to America. The Massachusetts House of Representatives urged people to boycott British goods. They asked other colonial assemblies to join their protests. Opposition to the British was spreading.

Intolerable Acts

A VIEW OF THE TOWN OF BOSTON WITH SEVERAL SHIPS OF WAR IN THE HARBOUR.

Boston was one of the busiest ports in colonial America. When the British shut it, they badly damaged colonial trade.

Following the Tea Party, with unrest growing in Boston, the British government responded swiftly. In 1774, Parliament passed what became known as the Coercive Acts, a series of laws intended to punish Massachusetts. The outraged Americans called them the "Intolerable Acts."

The laws included the Boston Port Act, which closed the harbor until the city paid the East India Company for the tea lost at the Tea Party. Other acts put Massachusetts under the control of British officials. The civilian governor was replaced by a soldier, General Thomas Gage.

Liberty Threatened

British soldiers took supplies from the militia, leaving the colonies without arms. British troops could be lodged in private houses, and any crime committed by a colonial official was now to be tried in England, not in Massachusetts.

THE QUEBEC ACT

Four of the Intolerable Acts were aimed directly at Massachusetts. The fifth, however, extended the boundaries of Britain's colony in Quebec in Canada and allowed Catholics to worship freely. That benefited the French settlers there. In America, patriots were suspicious that the act was passed at the same time as the others. Some feared the British might use French Canadians to enforce their rule in British America.

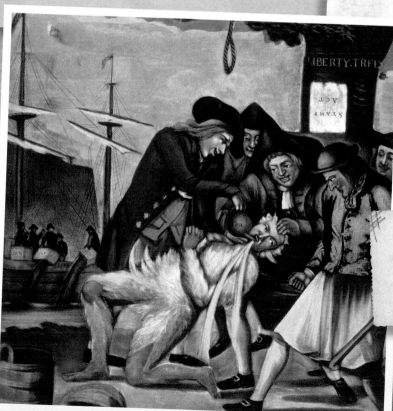

Patriots in Boston tar and feather a tax collector working for the British; they are forcing him to drink hot tea.

Continental Congress

The Continental Congress met for the first time in the Philadelphia State House in 1774. Twelve colonies sent representatives to discuss how to respond to the British government's Intolerable Acts. The meeting was the first step toward the creation of the United States of America.

The Continental Congress met at Carpenters' Hall in Philadelphia. The meetings were secret because they were illegal.

Samuel Adams was a Boston politician who first called for the Americans not to cooperate with the British government.

COLONIAL LEADERS

The men who led the campaign against the British were wealthy and educated. The First Congress included George Washington from Virginia, and John and Samuel Adams from Massachusetts. Benjamin Franklin and Thomas Jefferson joined the Second Continental Congress. Such men were motivated by a belief that every person had rights. Contemporary thinkers argued that if a government failed to protect these rights, people had the right to get rid of it.

Fifty-six deputies attended the First Continental Congress on September 5, 1774. Of the thirteen colonies only Georgia did not send a representative. Each colony attending had just one vote in proceedings, whatever its size.

A New Declaration

Meeting in secret, the representatives agreed on a declaration of colonial rights. The Congress proclaimed the colonists' right to life, liberty, property, assembly, and trial by jury. The proclamation later formed the basis of the Declaration of Independence. The Congress also criticized paying taxes to London when they had no say in how they were used, and objected to the presence of British troops in the colonies without Americans' consent. To show the British government they meant business, the Congress agreed on a trade boycott and a second congress.

The Second Meeting

The Second Continental Congress was held on May 10, 1775; this time, Georgia attended. Much had changed. The Americans had fought the British at the battles of Lexington and Concord and the British garrison in Boston was under siege.

The Congress immediately created an American army and appointed George Washington as its commander. In an effort to avoid full-scale war with the British, Congress sent an

By the KING,

A PROCLAMATION.

For suppressing Rebellion and Sedition.

GEORGE R.

WHEREAS many of Our Subjects in divers Parts of Our Colonies and Plantations in *North America*, misled by dangerous and ill-designing Men, and forgetting the Allegiance which they owe to the Power that has protected and sustained them, after various disorderly Acts committed in Disturbance of the Publick Peace, to the Obstruction of lawful Commerce, and to the Oppression of Our loyal Subjects carrying on the same, have at length proceeded to an open and avowed Rebellion, by arraying themselves in hostile Manner to withstand the Execution of the Law, and traitorously preparing, ordering, and levying War against Us. And whereas there is Reason to apprehend that such Rebellion hath been much promoted and encouraged by the traitorous Correspondence, Counsels, and Comfort of divers wicked and desperate Persons within this Realm: To the End therefore that none of Our Subjects may neglect or violate their Duty through Ignorance thereof, or through any Doubt of the Protection which the Law will afford to their Loyalty and Zeal; We have thought fit, by and with the Advice of Our Privy Council, to issue this Our Royal Proclamation, hereby declaring that not only all Our Officers Civil and Military are obliged to exert their utmost Endeavours to suppress such Rebellion, and to bring the Traitors to Justice; but that all Our Subjects of this Realm and the Dominions thereunto belonging are bound by Law to be aiding and assisting in the Suppression of such Rebellion, and to disclose and make known all traitorous Conspiracies and Attempts against Us, Our Crown and Dignity; And We do accordingly strictly charge and command all Our Officers as well Civil as Military, and all other Our obedient and loyal Subjects, to use their utmost Endeavours to withstand and suppress such Rebellion, and to disclose and make known all Treasons and traitorous Conspiracies which they shall know to be against Us, Our Crown and Dignity; and for that Purpose, that they transmit to One of Our Principal Secretaries of State, or other proper Officer, due and full Information of all Persons who shall be found carrying on Correspondence with, or in any Manner or Degree aiding or abetting the Persons now in open Arms and Rebellion against Our Government within any of Our Colonies and Plantations in *North America*, in order to bring to condign Punishment the Authors, Perpetrators, and Abettors of such traitorous Designs.

Given at Our Court at St. *James's*, the Twenty-third Day of *August*, One thousand seven hundred and seventy-five, in the Fifteenth Year of Our Reign.

God save the King.

LONDON:
Printed by *Charles Eyre* and *William Strahan*, Printers to the King's most Excellent Majesty. 1775.

Once fighting began in the colonies, George III issued this proclamation calling for the rebellion in America to be suppressed.

Thomas Jefferson was a delegate at the Second Continental Congress when he was asked to write the Declaration of Independence.

"Olive Branch" petition to King George III, but he refused to accept it. On July 2, 1776, the gradual move away from British rule ended with the irreversible step of the Congress breaking all ties. Two days later—on July 4—the Congress approved the Declaration of Independence, which spelled out American complaints against Britain.

Congress Continues

In the next years, as the Revolutionary War continued, the Second Continental Congress continued to work out how the new United States would govern itself. In May 1787, in response to the need for a framework for government, Congress called a convention to create a constitution for the new country.

THOMAS JEFFERSON

A member of the Congress and one of the Founding Fathers of the United States, Jefferson (1743–1826) was the main author of the Declaration of Independence. He believed that individual freedom was at the core of the American Revolution. After the creation of the United States, Jefferson served as secretary of state, vice president, and then president. He oversaw the Louisiana Purchase from France in 1803, adding a vast area to the country.

The British Army

British troops were drilled frequently so that they could move quickly in formal lines to take up positions for battle.

The British army had some 36,000 men at the start of the war, but many were posted around the world to defend Britain's empire. The British sent soldiers to occupy Boston in 1768. When fighting began, they sent reinforcements, but the government was confident the rebellion would quickly be over.

Some observers believe that Gage was sympathetic to the patriots; other British officers refused to serve in the war for the same reason.

When the war did not end quickly, the British hired soldiers from several German states, including Hesse. The Germans were referred to as "Hessians." The British also recruited loyalist Americans, who in 1779 formed five units called the American Establishment. By then the British had some 60,000 troops in America.

Changing Tactics

The British and Germans were trained in the kind of warfare common in Europe at the time. Their tactics were based on infantry who stood in lines to fire muskets at the enemy. Fighting in the forests of North America, this approach was of little use. As the war went on, the commanders used more light infantry, who could fight in smaller, more fluid groups. They arranged their troops in looser formations that allowed them to scramble around obstacles to get into position to fire.

THOMAS GAGE

The commander in chief of the British forces at the start of the war was General Thomas Gage. He was a veteran of the French and Indian War who was appointed as military governor of Massachusetts in 1774. Although he was initially popular with colonial Americans, his enforcement of the Intolerable Acts made him a target of much hatred. The British, meanwhile, criticized him for not controlling American groups who were calling for independence.

Patriots and Militia

Before the American Revolution, the British had encouraged the Americans to support regular British soldiers in defending the colonies. The population formed bands of citizen–soldiers, or militia. Now the Americans were getting ready to fight the British, many militia became patriots. They were like ready-armed soldiers.

A militia unit marches behind a fifer and a drummer. The men used the long guns they used for hunting on the frontier.

The militia system in the colonies required every white, able-bodied man to serve as a soldier when required. Only Pennsylvania, which was founded by pacifist Quakers, did not expect men to serve in the militia. The wealthy were able to pay a fine to avoid serving, so the militiamen tended to be from poorer families.

Loyalist or Patriot?

Most militia sided with the revolutionary cause before the war. Loyalists formed their own militia units or joined the British army. In fact, however, only four out of ten American soldiers were militiamen.

NATIVE AMERICAN ALLIES

Like other inhabitants of the colonies, Native Americans took sides in the Revolutionary War. They had their own issues: they wanted to protect their homelands and maintain access to trade and supplies. The Iroquois, Mohawk, Seneca, Onondaga, and Cayuga joined the British cause; the Oneida and Tuscarora joined the American side.

Colonial militia fight Narragansett warriors near Rhode Island in a clash called the Great Swamp Fight, in 1675.

The Minutemen

Minutemen were militiamen who could be ready to fight at short notice—which is how they got their name. The first company of minutemen was set up in Worcester County, Massachusetts in September 1774. As war became inevitable, many militias formed minutemen units.

Minutemen seize their weapons and leave home to fight as a rider warns them that their community is under threat.

The minutemen were often the youngest and fittest members of the militia. They were also eager supporters of the patriot cause. The colonists deliberately restructured the militia to remove loyalists from positions of command. One third of all militia became minutemen.

A Brave Force

The minutemen were the first patriots to fight. Massachusetts minutemen fought British troops at Lexington and Concord, despite being outnumbered. On the advice of the Continental Congress, Maryland, New Hampshire, and Connecticut set up their own forces, but they were short lived. As war began, the rapid response of the minutemen was no longer needed. The militia were incorporated into the Continental army.

LIFE ON THE FRONTIER

The militia were an important defense force as settlers pushed west across America. Groups of militia formed to protect scattered settlements from the constant threat of Native American attack. Men in the community grouped together to use their superior weapons to drive off attackers who often lacked any gunpowder weapons.

This statue representing the minuteman John Parker marks the spot in Lexington where the first shot of the war was fired.

The Midnight Ride

Paul Revere was a well-known Boston silversmith and engraver. He was one of the leaders of the city's patriot movement.

On April 16, 1775, patriot Paul Revere set off from Boston for the ride of his life. Riding along unlit roads at night could be dangerous, but Revere had to warn the colonists at Concord to hide their arms from the British. Two nights later, Paul Revere set out again. This time he and William Dawes went to warn the colonists that the British were on their way.

Paul Revere's first ride gave the patriots in Concord enough time to move their military supplies. His second ride—on April 18, 1775—was more urgent. British soldiers were on their way. But neither he nor Dawes reached their destination: they were arrested by a British advance guard.

A Second Ride

Another rider, Doctor Samuel Prescott, did reach Concord. That night some 700 British redcoats crossed Boston Harbor in boats with muffled oars and marched toward Concord. The patriots would be waiting.

PAUL REVERE

Paul Revere (1735–1818) was a Boston silversmith and patriot who had taken part in the Boston Tea Party. As chief rider for Boston's Committee of Safety, which kept a check on the royal government, he often carried messages to New York or Philadelphia. He also gathered intelligence about British soldiers and passed it to the patriots. After he was captured on April 18, he was forced to return to Lexington on foot.

Revere was made famous in a poem by the 19th-century British poet Henry Wadsworth Longfellow, "Paul Revere's Ride."

The Battle of Lexington

British redcoats (bottom) fire at militiamen at Lexington. Although it is called a battle, the clash was really just a skirmish.

The governor of Massachusetts, General Thomas Gage, had orders to prevent a colonial revolt. He sent 700 soldiers to seize military supplies stored at Concord. But the colonists had been warned by Paul Revere. The British were met at Lexington Green by 77 militiamen commanded by Captain John Parker.

Parker arranged his militiamen in ranks on the village green. He gave them a famous order: "Stand your ground; don't fire unless fired upon, but if they mean to have a war, let it begin here."

First Shots

The British ran onto the green and lined up in formation. Parker ordered his men to disperse, but before they could, a shot rang out. The redcoats responded by firing a volley and making a bayonet charge. The outnumbered Americans ran for cover, leaving eight dead and ten wounded. One British soldier was hurt. The horrified British commander ordered his men to stop firing and march on to Concord.

As the two sides faced each other, a British officer shouted, "Lay down your arms, you damned rebels." The firing began soon after.

THE SHOT HEARD 'ROUND THE WORLD

No one knows who fired the first shot at Lexington Green; both sides said the other fired first. The US poet Ralph Waldo Emerson later called it "the shot heard 'round the world." The fighting at Lexington marked a change in relations between people and their rulers everywhere. When the argument about America's relationship with Britain became violent, it suggested that other struggles against the established order could become violent, too.

The Battle of Concord

After the skirmish at Lexington, the British moved on to Concord. Already, however, the arms they were looking for had been moved to a safer place. And, unlike the 70 or so militia who had been at Lexington, at Concord some 400 armed patriots were ready for the 700 British redcoats.

Militia fire on the British redcoats in the early morning mist on Lexington Green, delaying the advance on Concord.

Militiamen prepare to leave their families to set off to join their colleagues at Concord or along the road back to Boston.

At Concord, the militia commander Colonel James Barrett withdrew over the Concord River. As the British searched for weapons, more militia arrived. When Barrett had enough men, he advanced toward the small British detachment left to guard the North Bridge.

Surprising Victory

The British retreated across the bridge, but in the confusion a shot rang out, followed by more. Then the militia fired a volley. To the colonists' amazement, the British ran off into the town. The British continued their search for arms and, after lunch, prepared to march back to Boston.

THE RETREAT TO BOSTON

The decision by the British to have lunch before leaving was a mistake. It gave militiamen time to take up positions along the road to Boston. Throughout the retreat, patriots fired on the redcoats from behind trees, stonewalls, houses, and barns. This kind of guerrilla warfare was the colonists' best tactic against the British soldiers, who were used to conventional warfare. At the end of the day, British losses were 273, compared to only 95 American dead.

The War Moves to Boston

Hand-to-hand fighting breaks out as the redcoats reach the American positions at the top of Breed's Hill.

Harassed all the way by the patriots, the British column retreated back into Boston. By next morning, some 15,000 American militia surrounded the city. They formed the basis of the new Continental army. The British were effectively besieged in Boston for over a year.

The 15,000 Americans surrounded 6,500 British regulars under the command of General Thomas Gage. In June 1775, when the Americans heard a rumor that Gage planned to occupy Bunker Hill, 1,200 patriots set out to stop him.

The Battle of Bunker Hill

The patriots positioned themselves on Breed's Hill, below Bunker Hill, on the night of June 16, 1775. When shelling failed to dislodge the American position, the British charged up Breed's Hill. They eventually overwhelmed the patriots, but the victory came at a high price: the British lost half their force.

UNDER SIEGE

The siege of Boston lasted from April 19, 1775, until March 17, 1776. For most of the time, it was a stalemate. Neither side wanted to attack. Then, on March 4, 1776, the American commander George Washington occupied Dorchester Heights, overlooking Boston. From there, he shelled the British with artillery brought from Fort Ticonderoga. Now that Boston could not be supplied or evacuated by ship, the British surrendered on March 17.

Compared with the disciplined British troops, the militia at Bunker Hill were a ragged force who even lacked uniforms.

The Continental Army

The Continental army was formed by the Continental Congress on June 14, 1775, to fight the war. The next day, George Washington was elected its commander in chief. During the Revolutionary War, Washington's force went from being an untrained rabble to a well-organized force capable of defeating the British in a traditional battle.

Continental soldiers prepare to resist a British attack with bayonets; as the war went on, the army became far more effective.

GEORGE WASHINGTON

Born into a rich Virginia family, George Washington fought on the British side in the French and Indian War (1754–1763) before joining the patriot cause. Over the course of the war, he turned the Continental army into a respected, professional, and disciplined army. Despite several early defeats, he ultimately defeated the British. At the end of the war, he became the first president of the United States.

George Washington was a veteran officer when the Revolutionary War broke out, and volunteered to lead the new army.

The men who formed the army were volunteers, like the Massachusetts militia who surrounded Boston. The other colonies were asked to contribute troops, too. These men saw themselves as "citizen-soldiers" who would fight only until the war was won.

Quota System

Conditions for the soldiers were hard. Desertion rates remained from 20 to 25 percent throughout the war. Over time, discipline and camp hygiene improved, although 10,000 soldiers still died from disease. To keep up the numbers, from 1777 each state had to send a set quota of men to join the Continental army.

The Declaration of Independence

The Declaration of Independence was signed by 56 delegates to the Continental Congress; they are now called the Founding Fathers.

The Declaration of Independence is the founding document of the United States of America. In it, Thomas Jefferson set out the reasons for the split between Britain and the thirteen colonies. The Continental Congress adopted it on July 4, 1776, now celebrated as Independence Day.

Jefferson wrote the declaration at the request of the Congress. He based it on the political ideas of the British philosopher John Locke. Instead of arguing that the

Delegates sign the declaration in the Pennsylvania State House, now known as Independence Hall.

colonists had rights as British citizens, it argued that all men were born with natural rights. It also maintained that a government had a contract with its citizens. If the government broke the contract, the citizens had the right to reject it.

A New Social Contract

Jefferson argued that Americans had been forced to revolt against the king because George III had not fulfilled his side of the contract between subject and ruler. In the new United States, he said, all men would be equally entitled to "life, liberty, and the pursuit of happiness."

COMMON SENSE

Jefferson's ideas were influenced by a thin pamphlet published in January 1776. In *Common Sense*, the English writer Thomas Paine argued that the Americans had to become independent in order to preserve their unique national character. He also argued that the new country should not be a monarchy but a republic. The book was hugely influential. It sold 500,000 copies in its first year alone. (Paine gave the money to the Continental army).

The Revolutionary War

Volunteers enlist for the Continental army at a rally. Recruiting and keeping soldiers was a major problem for the patriots.

The patriot defeat at Bunker Hill showed that George Washington faced a huge task in organizing the Continental army. Elsewhere, patriot efforts to secure Canadian support also failed. Early setbacks, however, did not prevent patriot morale being boosted by the Declaration of Independence in July 1776.

The British planned to send an army south from Canada toward New York. It would try to recruit loyalists on the way. If the army could seize New York, it would isolate New England from the other colonies. Meanwhile, another army would capture Charleston, South Carolina, and raise a loyalist army in the southern colonies.

A Patriot Crisis

The attempt to capture Charleston failed, but the British did capture New York. Morale in the Continental army fell and whole units deserted, but Washington won a morale-boosting victory at Trenton, New Jersey, in December 1776.

HARSH WINTER AT VALLEY FORGE

The Continental army spent the winter of 1777 in camp at Valley Forge, Pennsylvania. The men were exhausted, sick, and hungry. Nearly 2,000 died from disease. But Washington and his advisors drilled the troops to make them more disciplined. By spring 1778, the army was a far better fighting force than it had been before.

George Washington inspects his cold and tired troops at Valley Forge during the bitterly cold winter of 1777.

A First American Victory

The next year, the British in New York headed south to capture the patriot capital at Philadelphia. That meant they could not reinforce the army heading south from Canada. In June 1777 an American force defeated that isolated British army at the Battle of Saratoga. News of this success convinced France to enter the war on the side of the United States. The Americans badly needed their support. The Continental army suffered badly during the harsh winter of 1777–78 at Valley Forge, Pennsylvania.

By the later years of the war, the Continental army had become an effective fighting force, with its own uniforms and weapons.

The British general Lord Cornwallis surrenders to the American forces at Yorktown, Virginia, on October 18, 1781.

Victory for the New Country

In 1778 the tide turned for the patriots. A British campaign in the South cost so many casualties that they withdrew to Virginia to await reinforcements. The reinforcements were prevented by a French blockade off the coast. That allowed the patriots to drive the British into a trap at Yorktown, Virginia. On October 19, 1781, the British surrendered. The fight that had begun with small skirmishes at Lexington and Concord had led to the defeat of the British army—and the creation of the United States.

DEFEAT AT YORKTOWN

The British General Lord Cornwallis set up a naval base at Yorktown, at the southern end of Chesapeake Bay. The British built fortifications to protect them as they waited for reinforcements. When a French fleet blockaded the entrance to the bay, reinforcement became impossible. On land, the British were surrounded by American and French troops. Cornwallis had no choice but to surrender—ending British rule in the thirteen colonies.

TIMELINE

1760   George III becomes king of Britain.

1763   After the end of the French and Indian War, King George III issues a proclamation limiting British settlement in North America to the east of a line drawn through the Appalachian Mountains.

1765   The Stamp Act imposes taxes on legal documents and newspapers in the American colonies.

1766   The Stamp Act is repealed, mainly for reasons to do with British domestic politics.

Samuel Adams of Boston writes a letter urging patriots not to cooperate with the British.

1767   The Townshend Acts impose taxes on legal documents and newspapers in the American colonies.

1768   British troops arrive to put Boston under military government.

1770   In the Boston Massacre, British troops open fire on a hostile crowd, killing five protestors.

1772   Colonial leaders set up Committees of Correspondence to share ideas about the government of the colonies.

1773   Colonial Americans dressed as Mohawk Indians board an East India Company ship in Boston Harbor and throw its cargo of tea overboard. The "Boston Tea Party" is a protest against a new British tax being imposed on tea.

1774 The British Parliament passes the Coercive Acts to punish Massachusetts for the Boston Tea Party.

Some colonies set up Committees of Safety to monitor the activities of colonial governments.

The first company of minutemen is formed in Worcester County, Massachusetts. September: Representatives from twelves colonies meet at the First Continental Congress in Philadelphia to protest the Coercive Acts, which Americans dub the "Intolerable Acts."

1775 April 16: Paul Revere makes a night ride to warn militia that the British will search for their arms supplies.

April 18: On a second night ride, Revere is captured by the British.

April 19: The Battles of Lexington and Concord take place.
April 19: Boston is placed under siege by patriots.

June 15: George Washington is elected commander in chief of the new Continental army.

June 17: Victory at Bunker Hill costs many British casualties.

1776 March 17: The British in Boston surrender.

July 4: The Second Continental Congress adopts the Declaration of Independence.

December 25: Washington crosses the Delaware to seize Trenton.

1777 Washington's army survives a bitter winter at Valley Forge.

1781 Trapped at Yorktown, Virginia, and blockaded at sea by a French fleet, the British army surrenders, ending the war.

1783 The Treaty of Paris formally recognizes the United States of America as an independent nation.

GLOSSARY

bayonet A blade added to the end of a gun barrel as a stabbing weapon.

boycott An organized refusal to buy goods from a particular source.

coercive Using threats or intimidation to force people to act in a particular way.

congress A formal gathering of official representatives.

duty A tax added by governments to the price of goods, mainly imports.

empire A group of nations or peoples all ruled over by an emperor, empress, or other ruler.

governor An official appointed to govern a colony or territory on behalf of the government.

guerrilla warfare Fighting by tactics such as ambushes or raids, rather than traditional battles.

loyalist An American who supported the British during the revolution.

militia An army made up of civilians rather than professional soldiers.

minutemen Militiamen who were ready to fight at short notice.

morale The belief of a fighting force that it will eventually be victorious.

patriot An American who supported the revolutionary cause.

proclamation A declaration by a government that it has made a particular decision.

quota A required quantity.

siege A situation in which a town or force is entirely surrounded by the enemy and cannot receive supplies.

skirmish A minor battle between small forces.

tyrant A ruler who uses his or her power in a harsh or cruel way.

volley The simultaneous firing of many weapons.

FURTHER INFORMATION

Books

Brown Reference Group. *Battle Box: Revolutionary War*. Simon and Schuster Children's Publishing, 2009.

Catel, Patrick. *Battles of the Revolutionary War*. Heinemann Raintree, 2010.

Earl, Sari. *George Washington: Revolutionary Leader and Founding Father*. ABDO Publishing Company, 2010.

Micklos, John. *What Was the Revolutionary War All About?* Enslow Elementary, 2008.

Murphy, Daniel P. *The Everything American Revolution Book: From the Boston Massacre to the Campaign at Yorktown*. Adams Media, 2008.

Murray, Stuart. *American Revolution (Eyewitness)*. DK Children, 2005.

Websites

www.pbs.org/ktca/liberty/
Site to accompany the PBS series *Liberty! The American Revolution*.

www.bl.uk/onlinegallery/features/americanrevolution/index.html
British Library site that uses the library resources to explore the war.

www.shmoop.com/american-revolution/
Kids' guide to the Revolutionary War written by postgraduates from Harvard University.

www.historyplace.com/unitedstates/revolution/index.html
The History Place timelines of the Revolutionary War.

Publisher's note to educators and parents: Our editors have carefully reviewed these websites to ensure that they are suitable for students. Many websites change frequently, however, and we cannot guarantee that a site's future contents will continue to meet our high standards of quality and educational value. Be advised that students should be closely supervised whenever they access the Internet.